Jazz
GUITAR CHORD VOICINGS

By Arthur Rotfeld

T0088314

Cherry Lane Music Company
Director of Publications: Mark Phillips

ISBN: 978-1-57560-625-5

Contents

Editor's Note: The focus of this book is on harmony. Rhythmic notation is omitted to ensure emphasis on this purpose. The reader is encouraged to apply rhythmic ideas as soon as he or she is comfortable with the fingerings and concepts.

Introduction

Jazz Guitar Chord Voicings presents an overview of harmonic techniques available to the contemporary jazz guitarist. Learning every example will ensure a thorough and practical knowledge of jazz harmony.

The fundamental theory, including all you need to know about chord construction, is explained in an introductory chapter. In Chapter 1, a comprehensive overview of guitar voicings is presented. Play through this section to familiarize yourself with the sound palate of jazz, and consult it as a reference. You'll find that this section is filled with *useful* voicings and is a relief from exhausting chord dictionaries.

The most common chord progressions in jazz are presented in Chapter 2, so that you can learn the building blocks of jazz harmony with a multitude of great sounding voicings. A complete guide to chord substitution is given in Chapter 3; it expands on and illuminates what you've already learned in Chapters 1 and 2, so you can develop a thorough understanding of the jazz harmonic practice—the *how* and *why* of the jazz masters. *Jazz Guitar Chord Voicings* culminates with the musical application of all the material in standard-based progressions.

Make an effort to apply all of these concepts and your newfound knowledge to your musical situations, and you will meet with remarkable success.

Arthur Rotfeld

About the Author

Arthur Rotfeld is a guitarist, composer, and teacher. He received bachelor degrees in education and jazz studies from the University of Bridgeport, and earned a Master of Fine Arts in composition from the Conservatory of Music at SUNY Purchase, where he also taught solfège. He is a private instructor of guitar, bass, and piano, and he also teaches music at New York area colleges. Arthur spent five years as the educational music editor at Cherry Lane Music, where he wrote and edited numerous instructional guitar books. His work has appeared in various print and on-line magazines. Arthur lives in White Plains, NY, and he performs regularly in the New York metropolitan area. Visit him on the web at www.rotfeld.com.

Chapter 1: Harmony Fundamentals

Scales and Chord Formulas

Chord construction is often discussed using numbers and formulas. These numbers invariably are tied to degrees of major scales. The notes of a scale are assigned numbers in consecutive order. A sharp (♯) or flat (♭) in a formula tells us that a certain note needs to be raised or lowered respectively by a half step. For example, the major chord formula is 1–3–5, which tells us that we need the root (1st), 3rd, and 5th of the major scale to build the chord; the minor chord formula is 1–♭3–5, which tells us we need the root, ♭3rd, and 5th of the major scale to form the chord.

Here is a two octave C major scale, labeled with Arabic numerals:

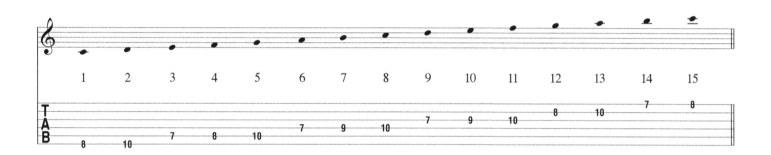

Here is a chart showing some basic chord types:

Chord	Formula
Major	1–3–5
Minor	1–♭3–5
Diminished	1–♭3–♭5
Augmented	1–3–♯5
Major Seventh	1–3–5–7
Minor Seventh	1–♭3–5–♭7
Dominant Seventh	1–3–5–♭7
Diminished Seventh	1–♭3–♭5–♭♭7
Augmented Seventh	1–3–♯5–♭7

Chord Symbols

Chord symbols are not entirely standardized; the way that they are written varies from musician to musician—and from publisher to publisher. The chart below shows many common chord types and the symbols we'll use, plus the various other ways you might see them (notated in parenthesis).

Chord	Symbol	
C major	C	(CM, Cmaj, C$^\triangle$)
C minor	Cm	(Cm, C−)
C major seven	Cmaj7	(CM7, C$^\triangle$7)
C minor seven	Cm7	(Cm7, C−7)
C dominant seven	C7	
C diminished seven	C°7	(Cdim7)
C augmented seven	C7$\sharp$5	(C7+5, C+7, Caug7)
C minor seven flat five	Cm7♭5	(C$^\varnothing$, C$^\varnothing$7)
C seven sharp nine	C7$\sharp$9	(C7+9, C7−10)

Harmonized Scales

Chords are closely related to scales. In fact, nearly all chords can be generated by stacking notes, a 3rd apart, above each scale degree. Studying harmonized scales serves two purposes. First, we can learn what different *chord qualities* sound like (such as major 7th or minor 7th). Second, we can learn what chords built on each *scale degree* sound like (such as what a minor 7th chord sounds like when built on the 2nd degree, compared to one built on the 3rd degree).

Here are two versions of a harmonized C major scale:

1. Tightly voiced chords. This is a way that a pianist would voice them.

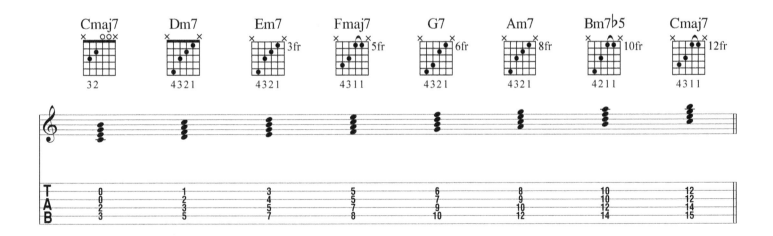

2. Loosely voiced chords. This is a more guitar-friendly way to voice them.

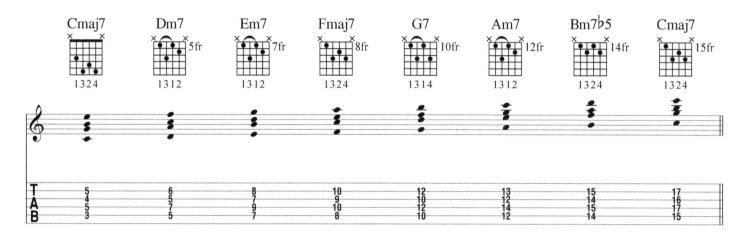

Here are two versions of a harmonized C harmonic minor scale:

1. Tightly voiced chords. This is a way that a pianist would voice them.

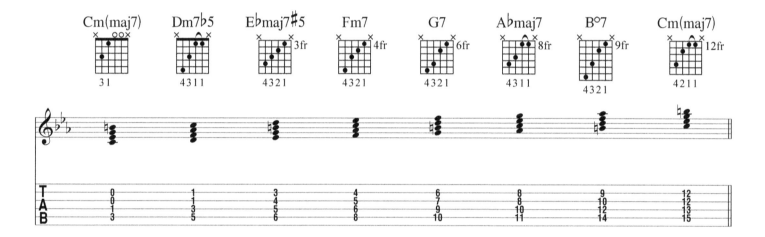

2. Loosely voiced chords. This is a more guitar-friendly way to voice them.

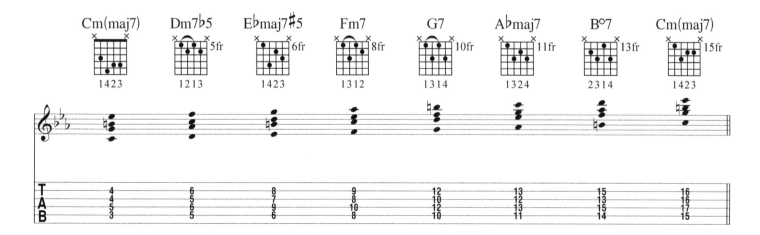

Chord Functions and Roman Numerals

Chords have functions in *tonal music* (music with a key center). Some chords sound stable and grounded, while others sound unstable and need to resolve. Labeling chords with Roman numerals helps us to understand how a chord is functioning. For example, the I chord is stable and sounds like "home"—in other words, it makes for a convincing ending chord. Other chords, such as the V, push ahead and want to move toward stability. Some chords, such as the ii or IV, fall in the middle ground. You will learn more about these inclinations by playing and reading about the progressions in this book. If you are a more scholarly type, you can also consult a harmony textbook.

This all might sound very dry and academic, but it's actually very practical and common—even in the vocabularies of untrained musicians. Maybe you've heard a musician say, "Let's play this song; it's a I–IV–V in A." This tells you that the song uses A (I), D (IV), and E (V) chords.

Here are the harmonized major and minor scales, presented with the names of each chord function and the Roman numeral analysis. Note that lowercase numerals represent minor or diminished chords and that uppercase numerals represent major or augmented chords. All of this information should be committed to memory.

This is the harmonized major scale:

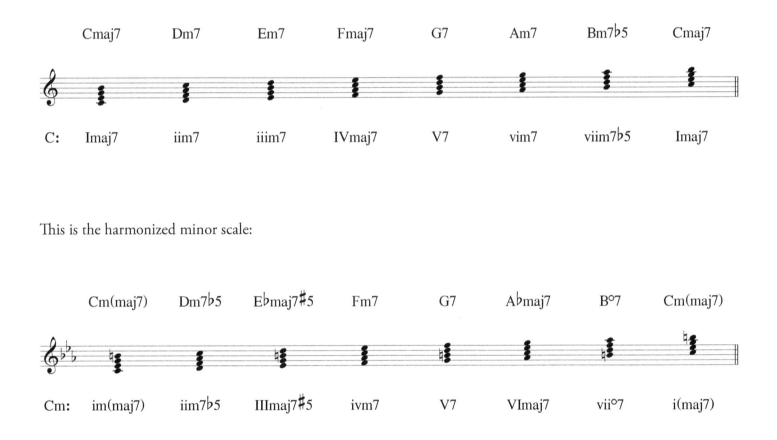

This is the harmonized minor scale:

Chapter 1: Harmony Fundamentals

7

Chapter 2: Chord Voicings

This chapter highlights numerous chord voicings. Here you'll find the most common chord qualities in their best sounding and most practical guitar fingerings. The root is always C, and all of the voicings are shown in root position—that is, the lowest note is the root. All of the chords are moveable, so try them with a number of different roots. After you become familiar with these voicings, experiment with leaving out the roots for a more modern, leaner sound. Take the time to analyze each chord tone and learn which is the 3rd, 5th, 7th, and so on.

Major Chords

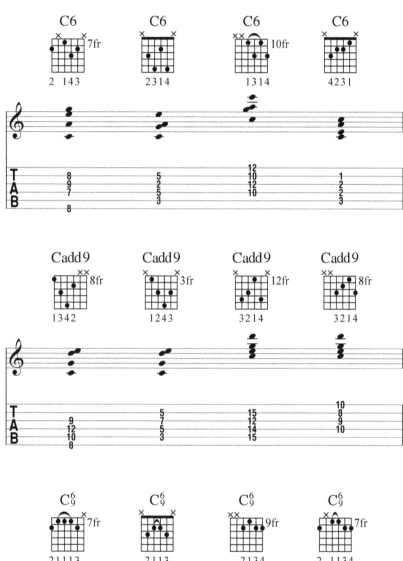

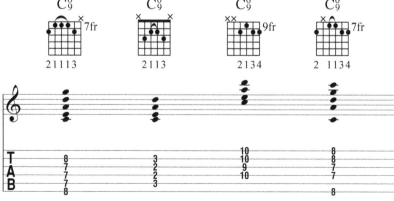

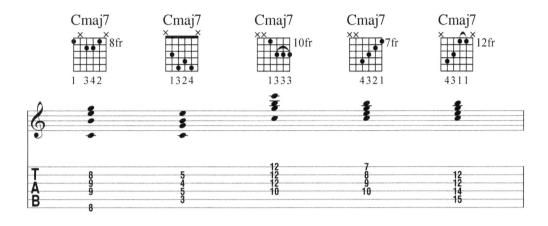

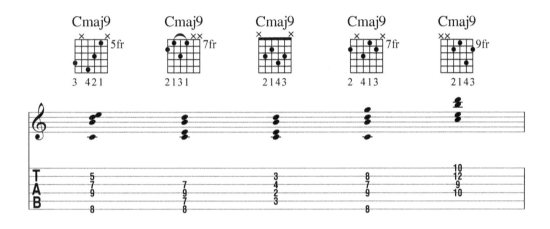

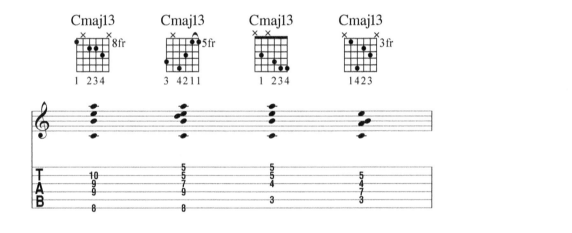

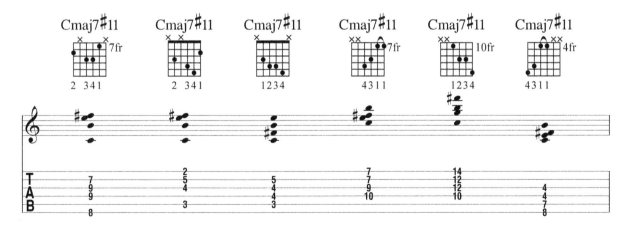

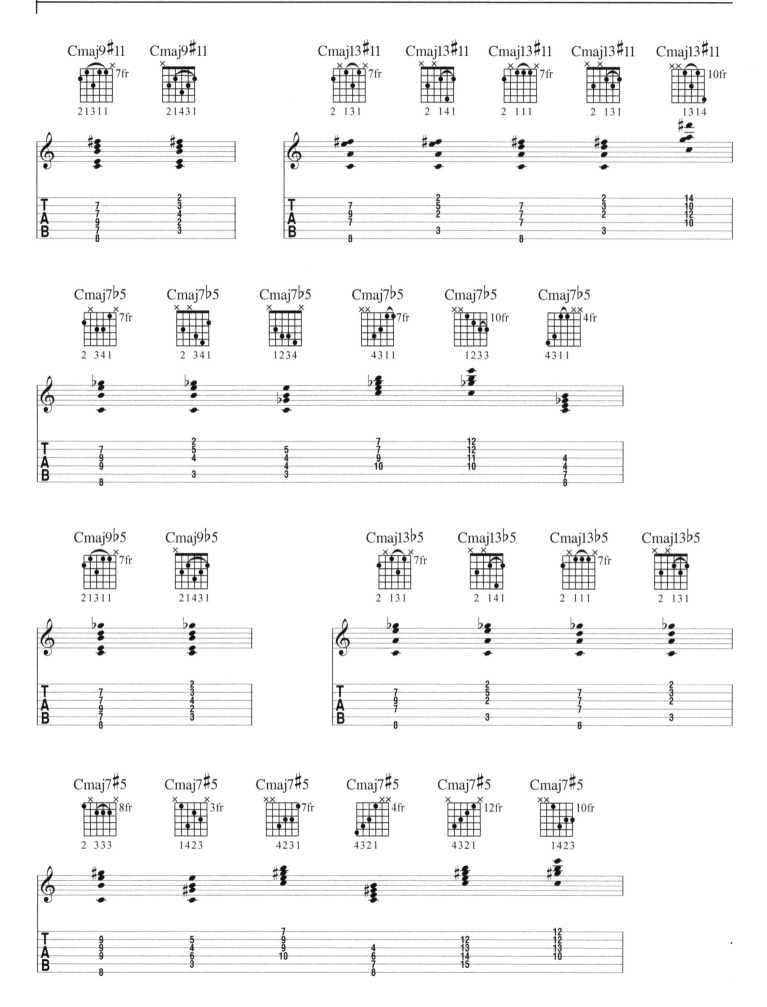

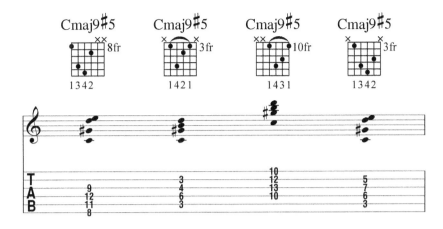

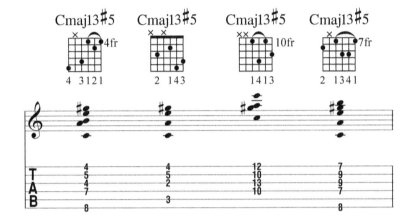

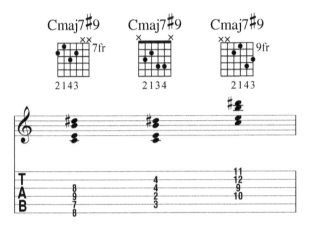

Minor Chords

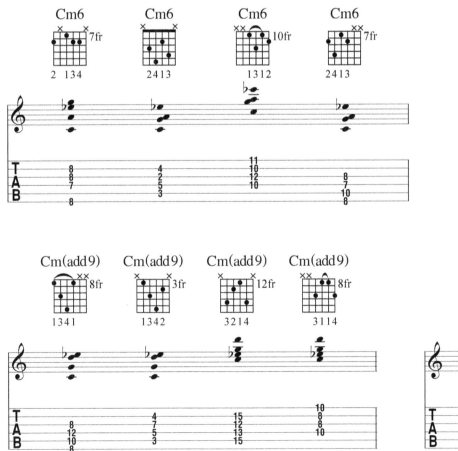

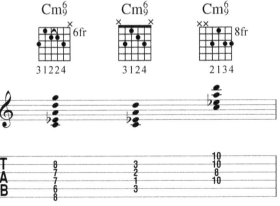

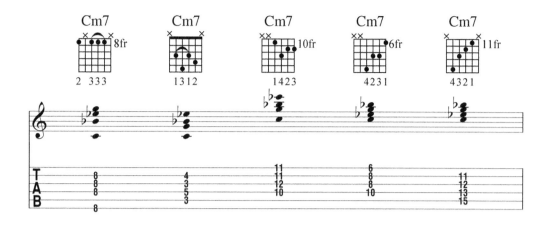

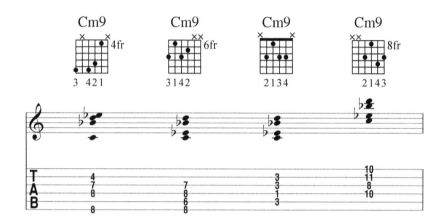

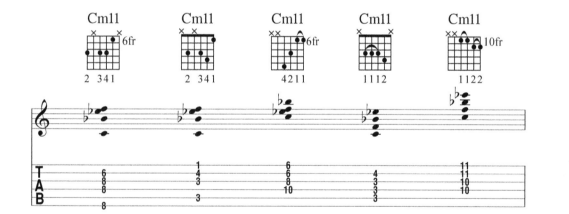

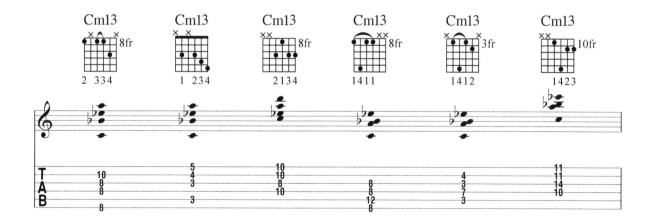

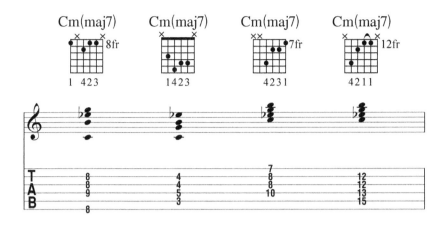

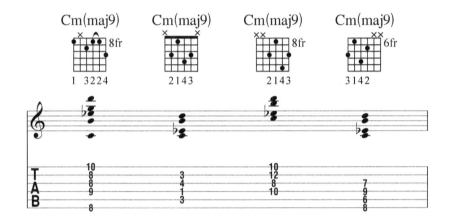

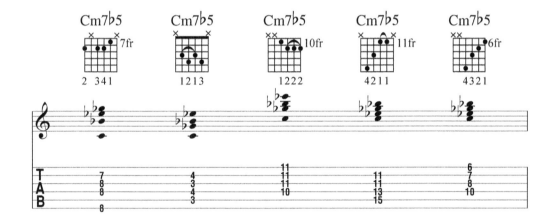

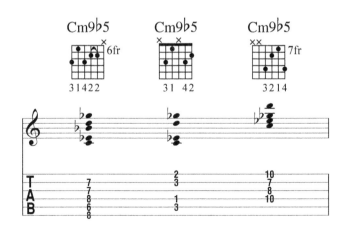

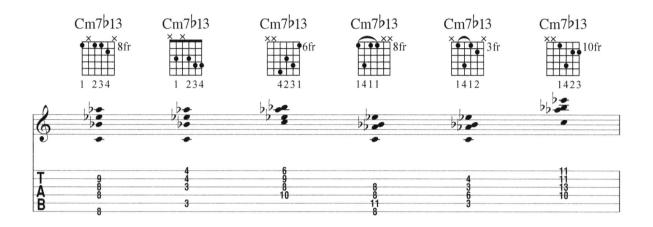

Dominant-Type Chords

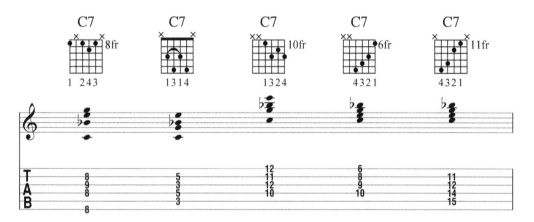

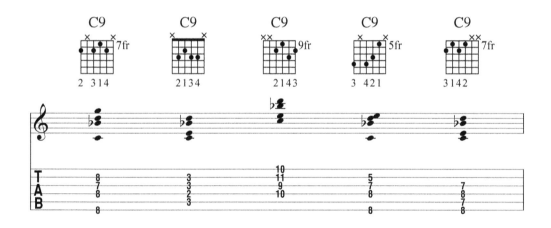

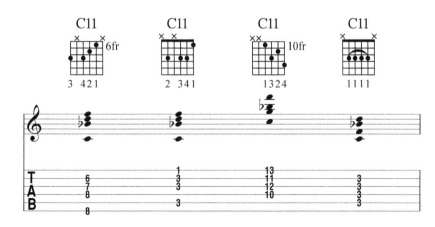

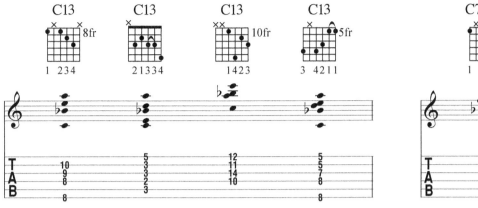

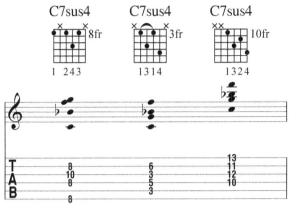

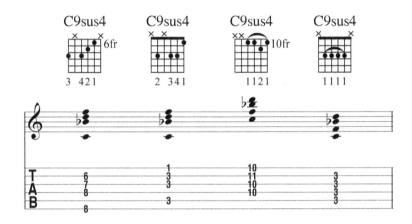

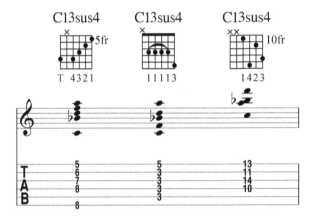

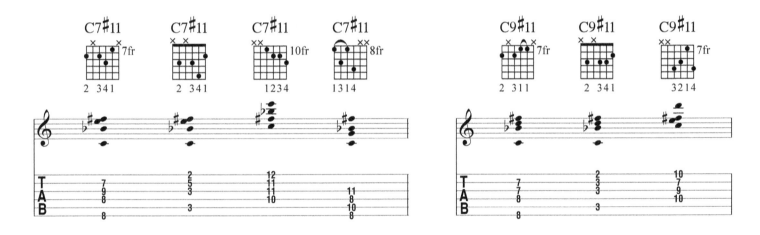

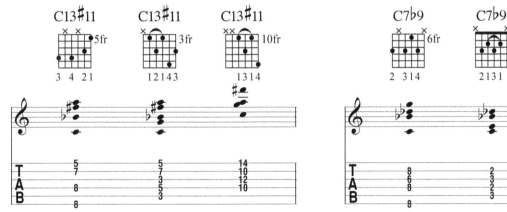

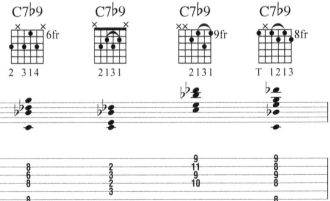

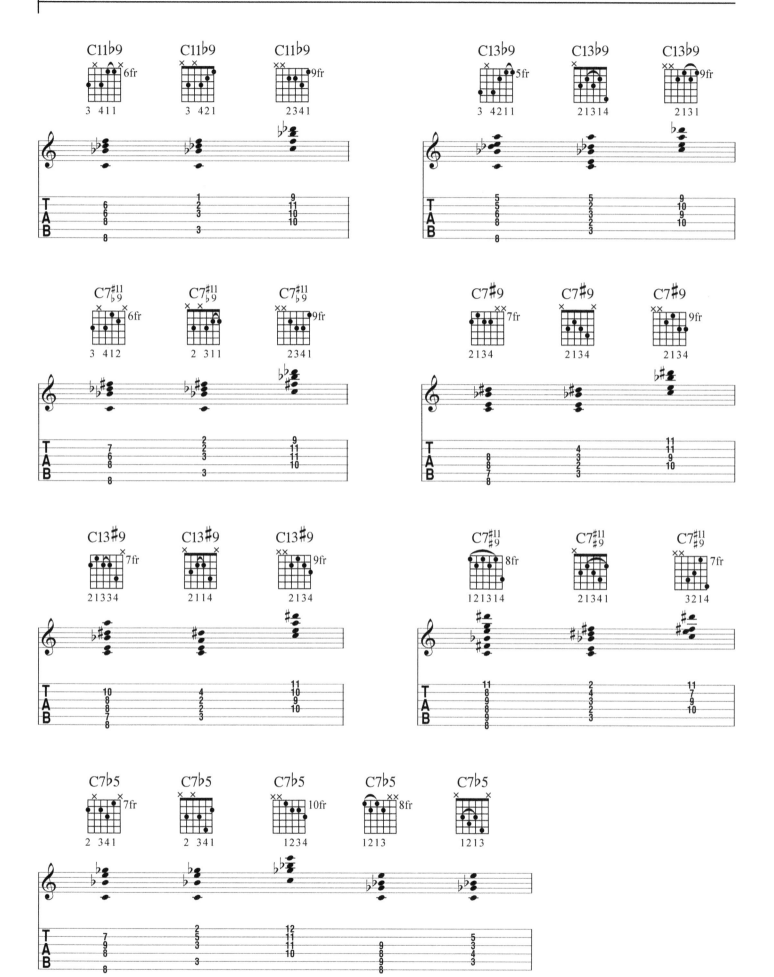

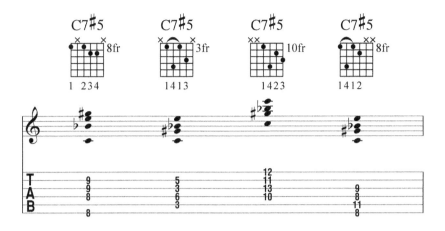

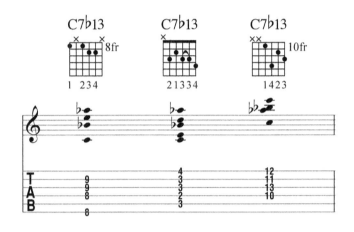

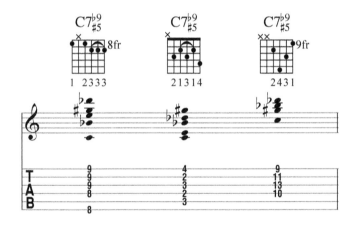

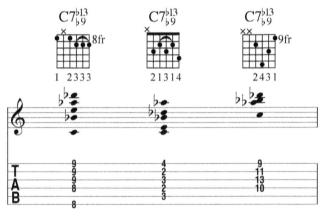

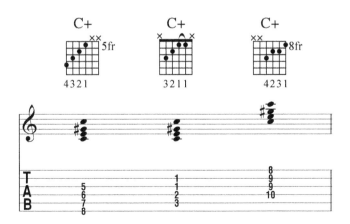

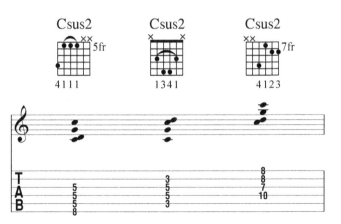

Other Chords

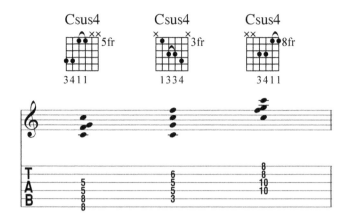

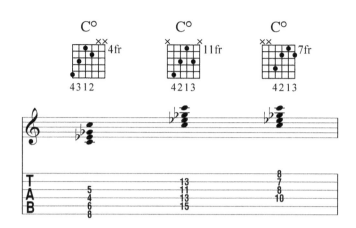

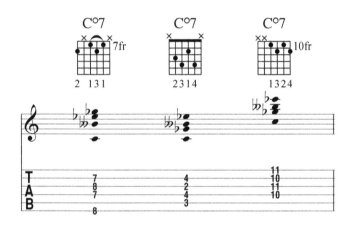

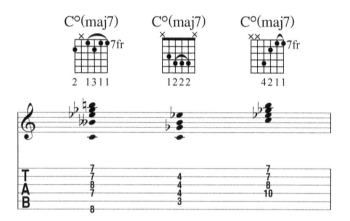

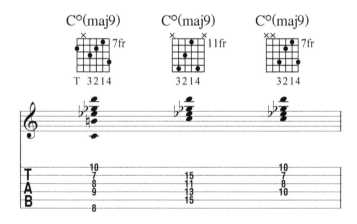

Chapter 3: The Progressions

The most common progressions in jazz, found in most standard tunes, are the ii–V–I and the I–vi–ii–V. We will explore the variations of these progressions that are used nearly all the time in jazz.

The progressions shown here use a multitude of variations in voicing, including four possibilities for each. The first two examples demonstrate how to apply the most common guitar voicings—the kind all beginning jazz guitarists learn—in a full, robust setting. The third example uses rootless voicings on the top four strings. The fourth example uses rootless chords in a tightly voiced, pianistic style.

Extensions and alterations are applied in numerous ways, and a wide variety of substitution techniques are used to ensure that you acquire a professional-level chordal style. Detailed explanations on extensions, alterations, and substitutions are discussed in Chapter 4.

Since most chord types are used (tonic major and minor, supertonic minor, and dominant), you will be prepared to handle almost any progression you encounter in the jazz repertoire. All of these examples are movable, so make efforts to learn them in as many keys as possible.

ii–V–I

iim7–V7–Imaj7

The iim7–V7–Imaj7 progression is the simplest building block of many standard jazz progressions. These three chords are *diatonic* (no chromatic alterations have been applied). They come straight from the harmonized major scale. Feel free to use 6, 6/9, or other major chords interchangeably. Extensions (including 9ths, 11ths, and 13ths) have been added to many chords for a jazzier sound, rather than using the more basic 7th chords.

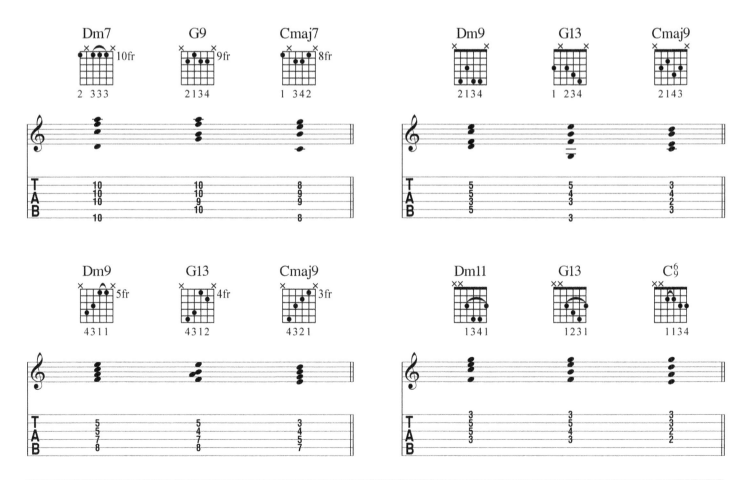

iim7–V7alt.–Imaj7

The second chord of the ii–V–I progression has been altered in this example. An alteration always involves chromaticism, which imparts a more colorful sound to the basic progression. Even though notes from outside the key are used, the sound is still firmly rooted in C. You may even find that the pull of the V chord is stronger now. Note that the Db7 in the second example is a substitute for the altered G7 chord. This is called the tritone substitution and is discussed in *Substitution Rule 6* on page 45.

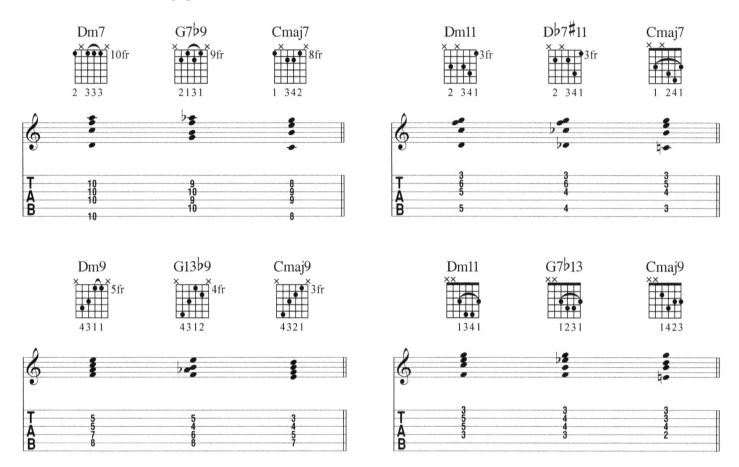

iim7b5–V7alt.–Imaj7

Here, the first two chords of the progression are altered. Essentially this is a ii–V in a minor key that resolves to a major chord. This is common practice in standard tunes, including many of those by Cole Porter, and in the off-the-cuff–type substitutions improvised by jazz musicians.

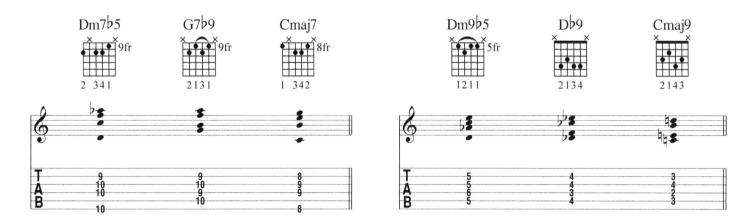

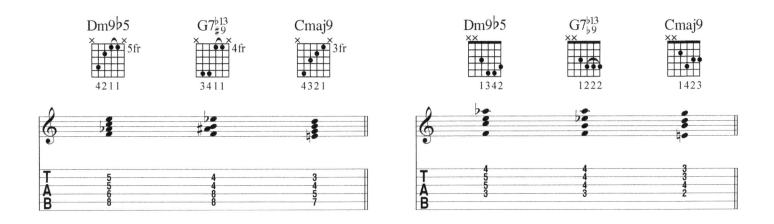

II7–V7–Imaj7

The first chord acts as the dominant of the dominant: the V of V chord. This chromaticism enhances the gravitational movement toward the dominant, and in turn, toward the tonic.

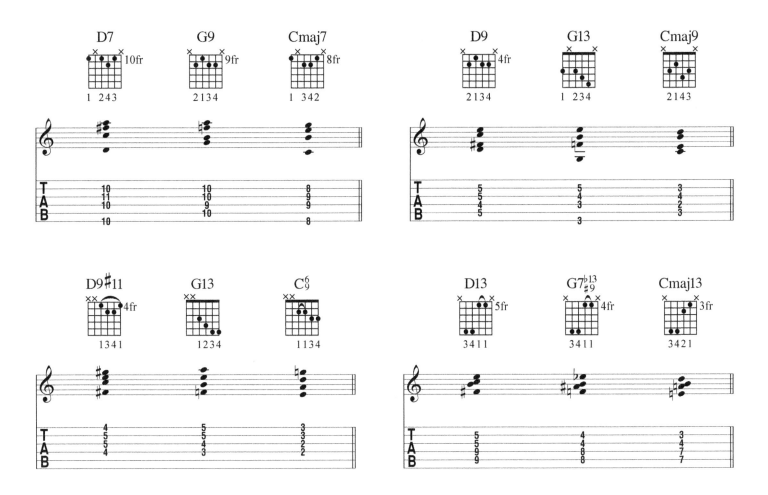

Coltrane Changes: ii–V/♭VI–♭VI–V/III–III–V–I

Jazz legend John Coltrane is probably the most important figure in the art of re-harmonization. His re-workings of earlier standards and bebop classics (such as "Body and Soul," "How High the Moon," "Confirmation," and "Tune Up") have been the source of agony and ecstasy for all jazz musicians since. Here, Coltrane goes beyond the typical rules of re-harmonization and alters the framework of the ii–V–I itself. This progression is based on a cycle of descending major 3rds (A♭, E, and C). Each of these chords is preceded by its respective dominant. Apply this progression judiciously.

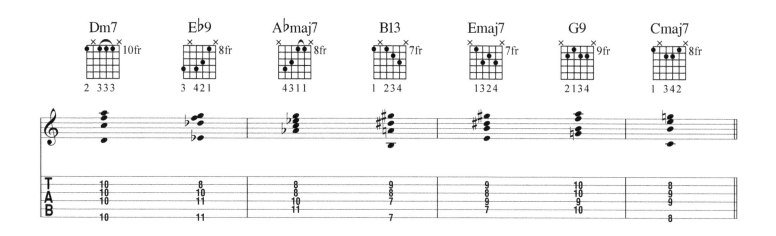

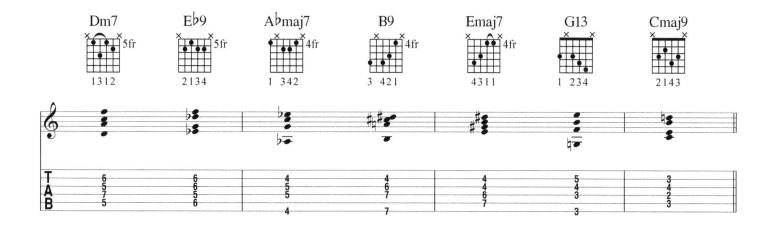

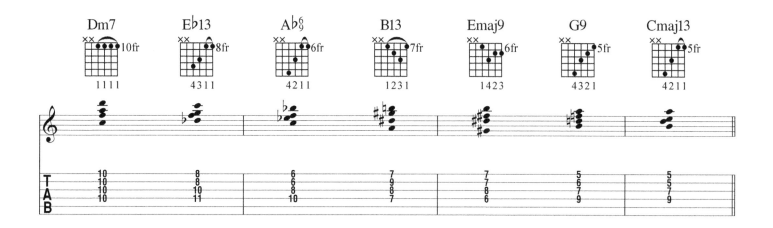

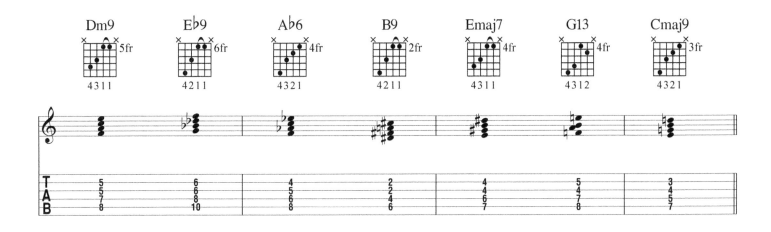

ii–V–i

iim7♭5–V7alt.–im7

This is the most common ii–V in minor. Minor keys are somewhat limited in the chord possibilities that lead to the tonic. The ii and V chords are usually harmonic minor-based, but the V chords in the second and fourth examples are from the G altered dominant scale (G–A♭–B♭–C♭–D♭–E♭–F). A special note about the tonic in minor: For a more stable sound many players prefer m6, m6/9, or even m(maj7) chords to act as the tonic in minor, instead of the m7 chord. The reason is that the m7 chord is from the modal-sounding natural minor scale (or Aeolian mode), while the m6 and the other minor types are from the tonal scales of the harmonic and melodic minor.

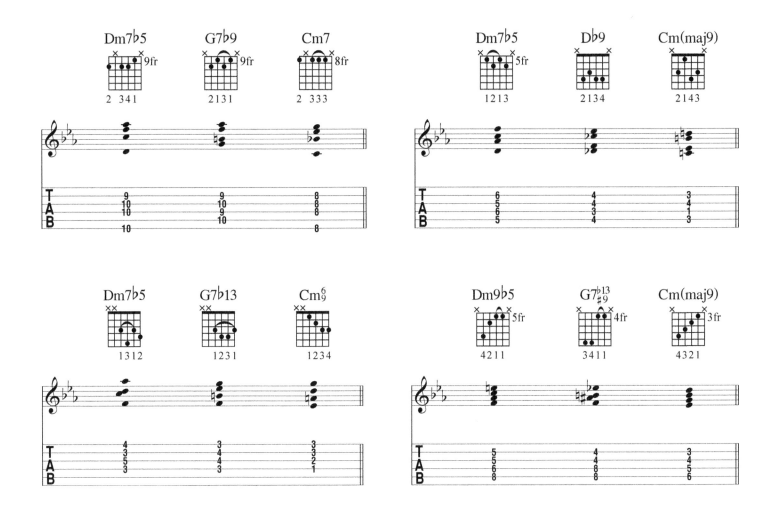

V7/V–V7–im7

The V of V works in minor as well as major. The II chords tend to have ♭9ths to stay closer to the minor tonality (natural 9ths on II chords imply a major tonality). Again, a variety of minor tonics are employed to accustom your ear to the different sonorities.

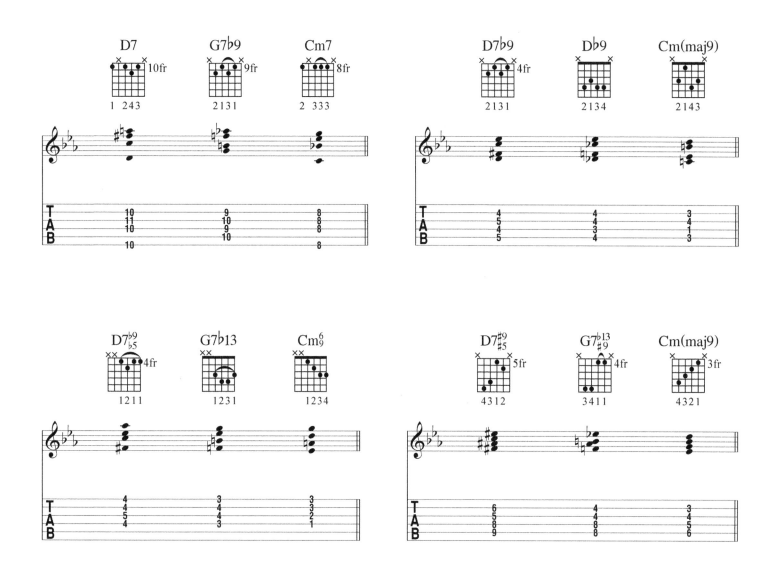

I–vi–ii–V

Imaj7–vim7–iim7–V7

The Imaj7–vim7–iim7–V7 is another building block of many standard jazz progressions. This progression occurs as the turnaround in the final two bars of most standards and jazz blues progressions. It is also the basis for *rhythm changes* (the chord changes of the Gershwins' "I Got Rhythm").

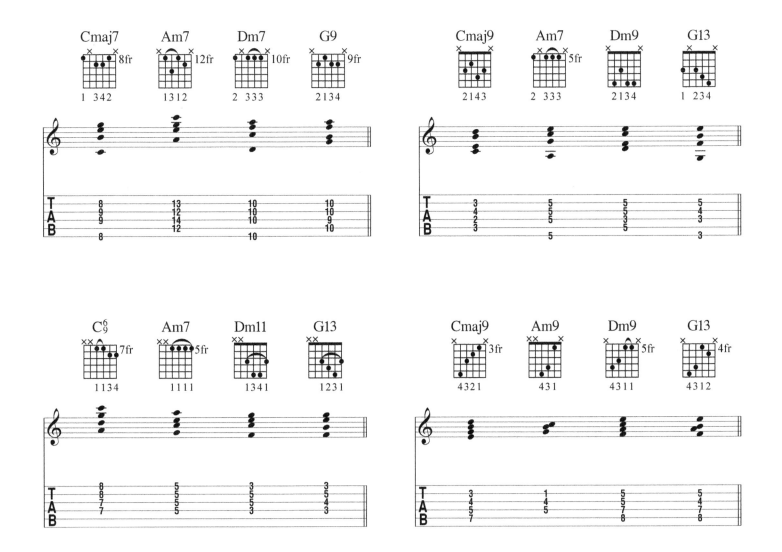

Imaj7–VI7alt.–iim7–V7

Because the ii chord is minor, it is best to alter the dominant that precedes it. Listen to soloists—they frequently imply this change in their lines. Many bebop players substitute these changes when they see the I–#I°7–ii–V progression.

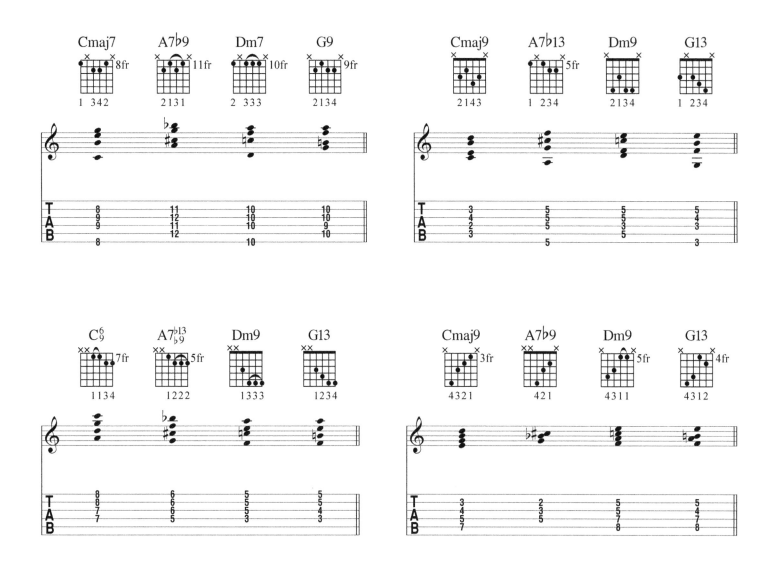

Imaj7– VI7alt.–iim7–V7alt.

This variation uses an altered dominant at the end of the progression.

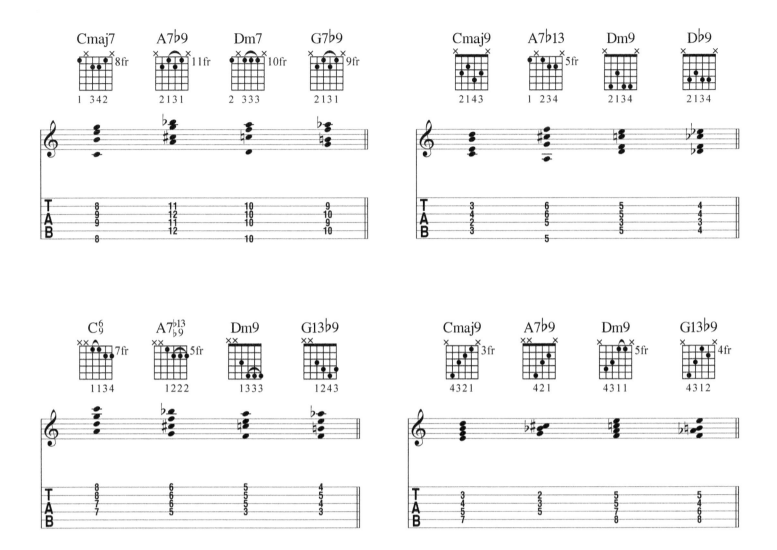

Imaj7–VI7alt.–V7/V–V7alt.

Dominants reign supreme here. This is like the previous examples, but with a V of V in place of the ii chord. The V/V is best left unaltered, but feel free to add extensions.

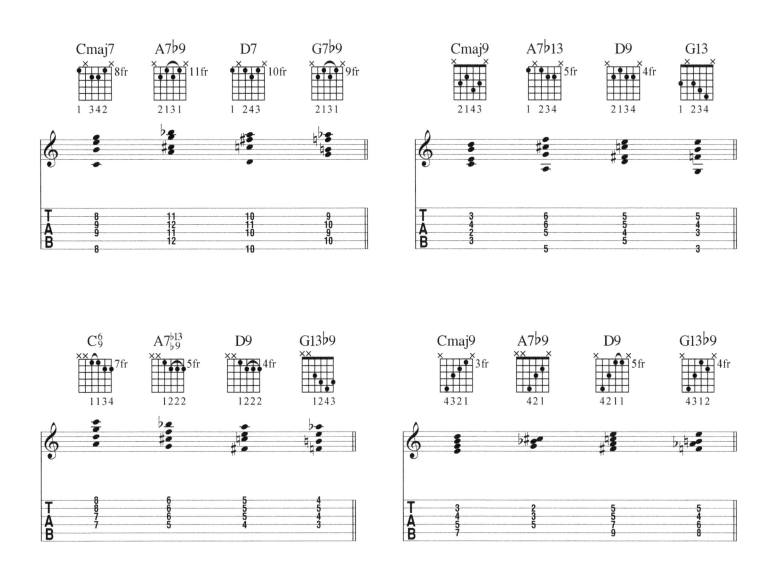

Imaj7–♭iii°7–iim7–V7

This progression is a holdover from the swing era. Here a ♭iii°7 is used to lead to the ii chord. It sounds even better when you precede it with a I chord in first inversion (with the 3rd in the bass), or substitute a iiim7.

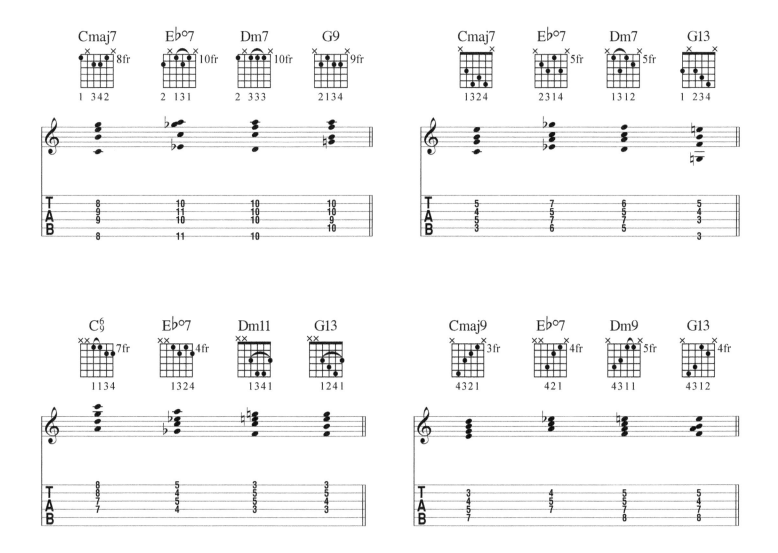

iiim7–vim7–iim7–V7

This is the first of many I–vi–ii–V progressions that substitute a iii chord for the I chord. This progression works even when the bass player plays a more conservative I–vi–ii–V line.

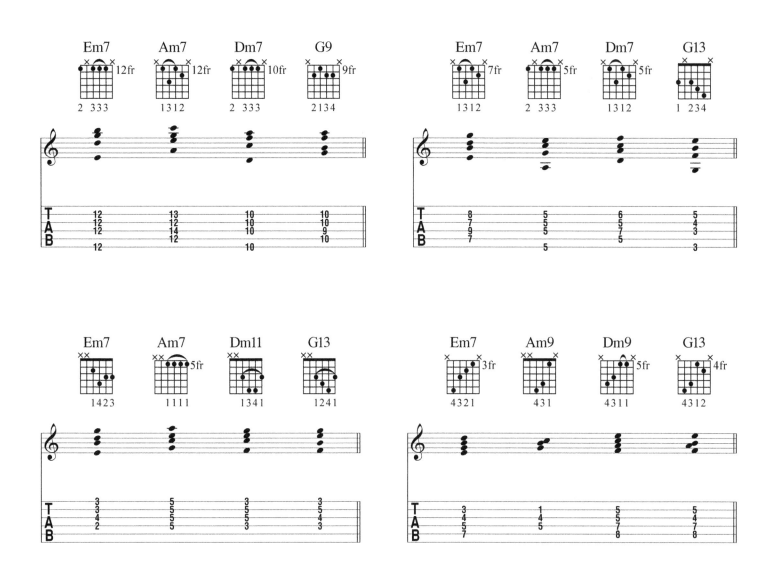

iiim7–♭iii°7–iim7–V7

The ♭iii°7 is a logical choice to place between the iii and ii for a smooth, chromatic descent.

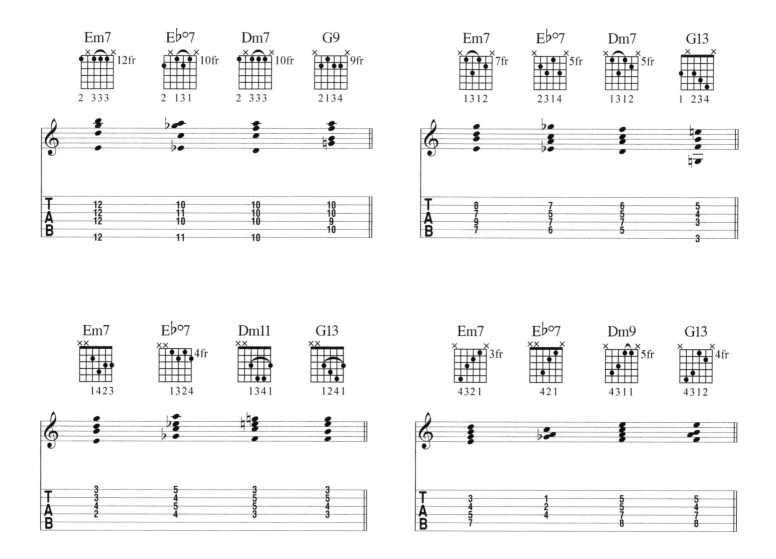

iiim7–VI7alt.–iim7–V7alt.

This is a common variation, ideal to use when comping for a bebop soloist.

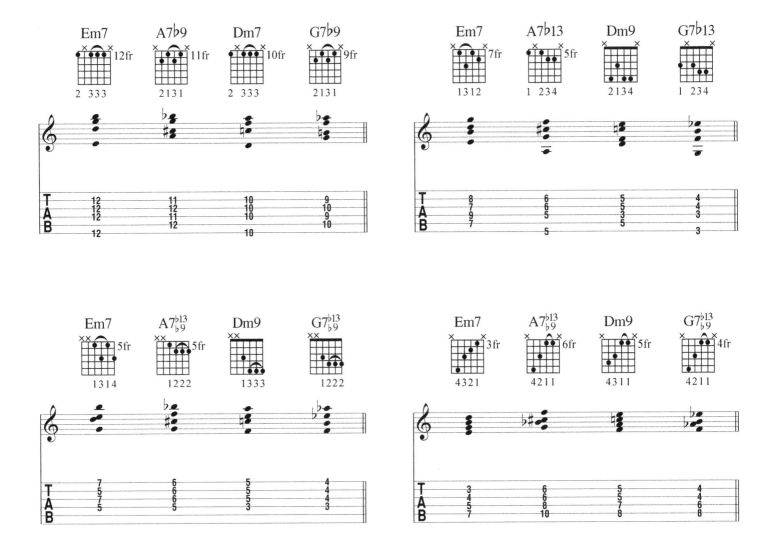

Imaj7–♭IIImaj7–♭VImaj7–♭IImaj7

This progression occurs in many bop and post-bop tunes by Thelonious Monk, Miles Davis, and John Coltrane. It's not often used as a I–vi–ii–V substitute in the body of rhythm changes–type tunes, but it is popular as a turnaround figure.

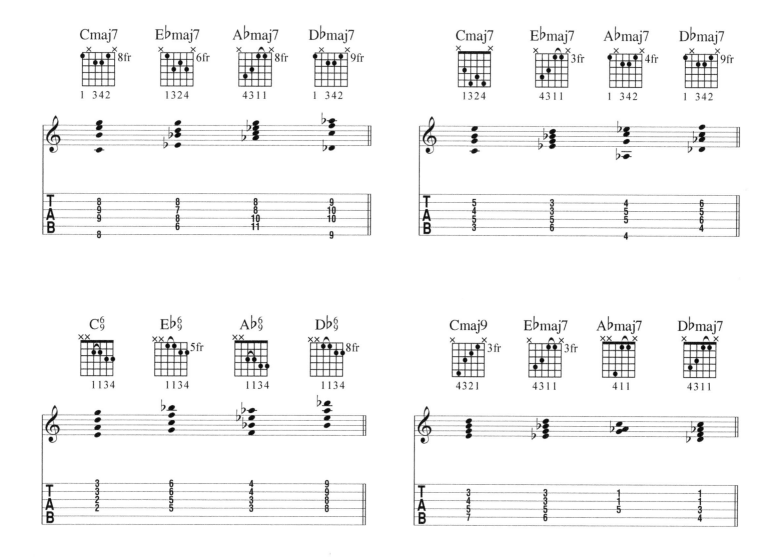

i–VI–ii–V

im7–♭VImaj7– iim7♭5–V7alt.

The minor i–VI–ii–V progression is not as common as its major counterpart, but that's probably because of the rhythm changes phenomenon. Frankly, this minor progression could be used more often than it is, so forge ahead!

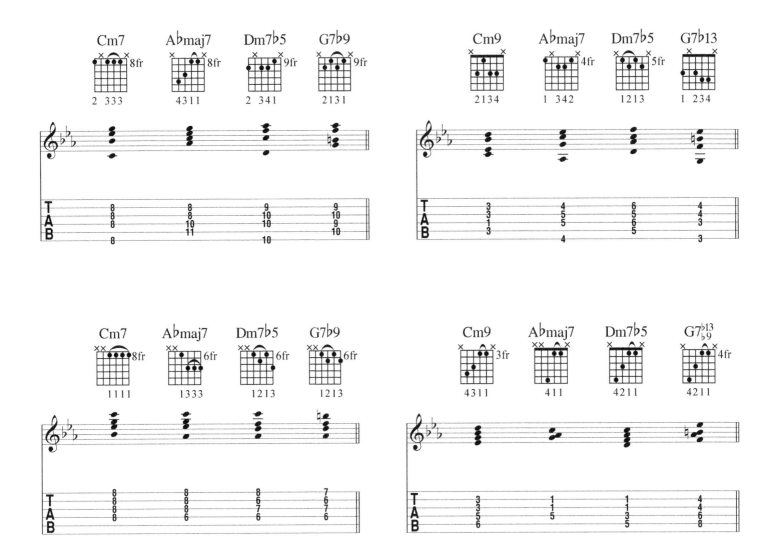

im7–VI7alt.– iim7♭5–V7alt.

Here, the VI7alt. chord is a bit surprising, but it will work well in soulful, post-bop settings—think '60s-era Horace Silver or Herbie Hancock.

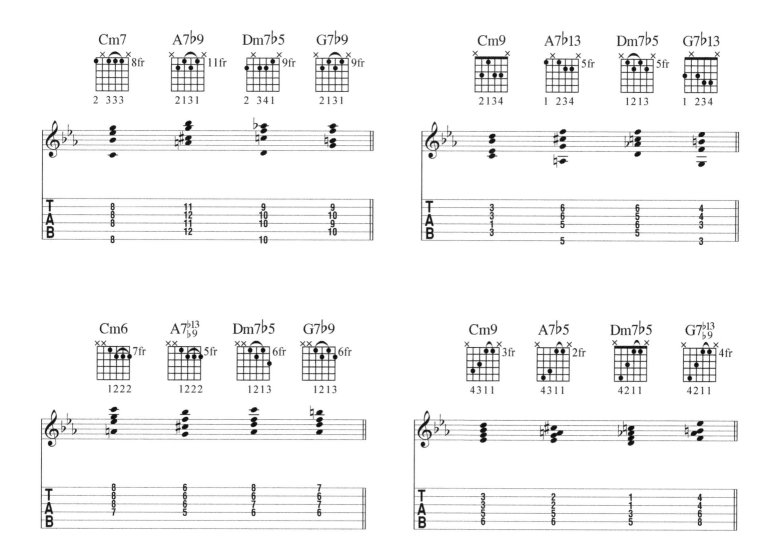

im7–vim7♭5– iim7♭5–V7alt.

The second chord of this progression sounds like a tonic m6 chord with the 6th in the bass. The progression uses a vi chord from the melodic minor scale, and the ii and V chords are from the harmonic minor scale.

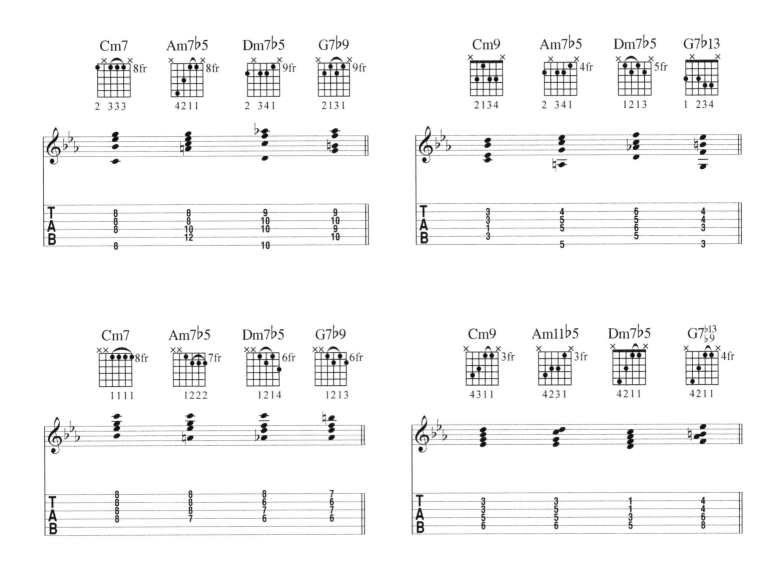

Dominant Cycles

V7/iii–V7/vi–V7/ii–V7

This is a cycle of dominant chords. Strings of chords like these are common and make for easy modulations to other keys. This particular progression (III7–VI7–II7–V7) is used in the bridge of rhythm changes, but dominant cycles are common in many other contexts as well.

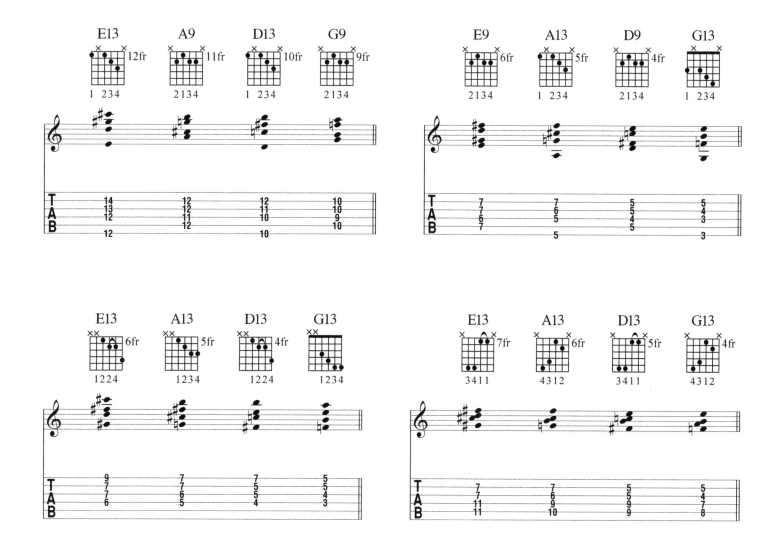

V/iii–Valt./vi–Valt/ii–V

Altered dominant chords are used here to create a smooth chromatic movement. This is a safe substitute—it will work well under most solo lines.

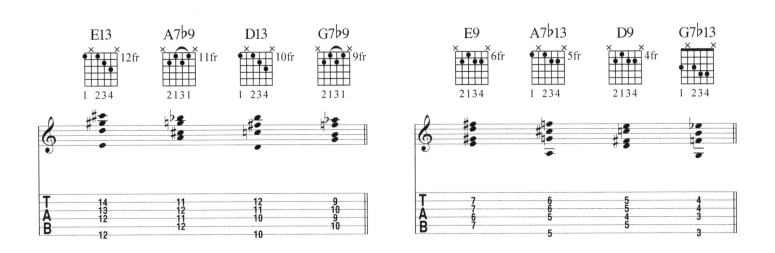

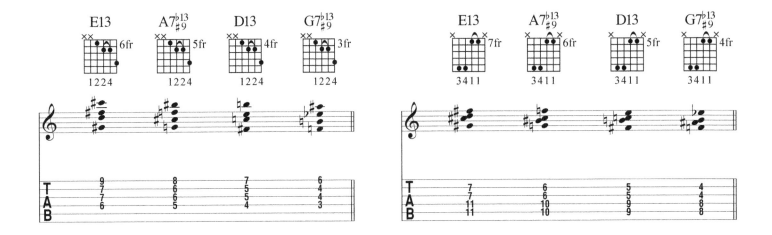

Further Development

The following examples demonstrate just two possible ways to expand on the stock progressions we've been working with. Use these progressions to spark your own creativity.

iim7–V7alt.–Imaj7 with Cool Chromatic Moves

A different starting voicing and tritone substitution are used to make for the smoothest possible movement between chords. Experiment with other voicings and make up some variants of your own, too.

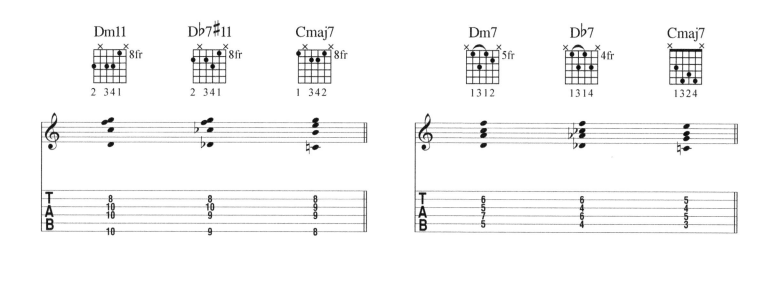

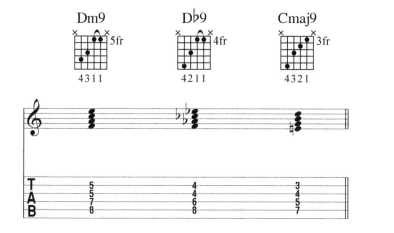

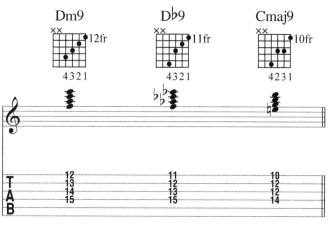

iim7–V7–V7alt.–Imaj7 with Cool Chromatic Moves

Moving from an unaltered dominant to an altered dominant is another way to make for the smoothest possible movement between chords. This example presents a subtler result because the movement takes place through an additional chord. The idea is to move as little as possible from one chord to the next—just enough to make the change. Try a similar approach by moving from iim7 chords into iim7♭5 chords.

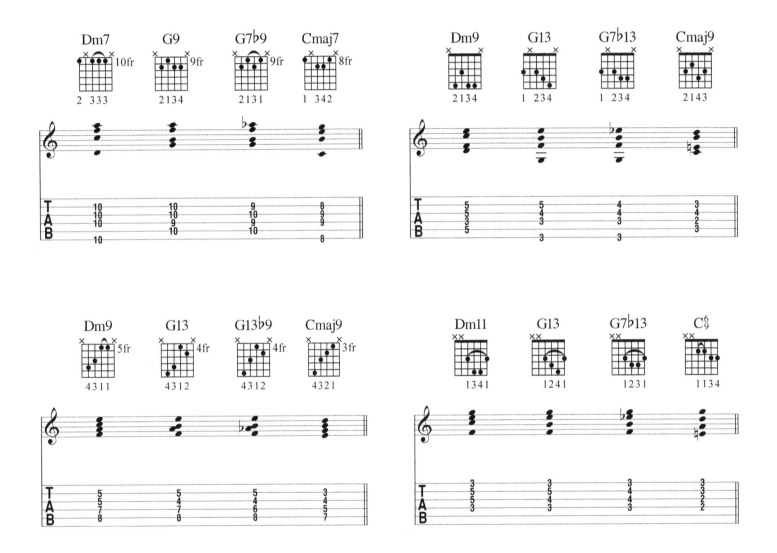

Chapter 4: Chord Substitution

We've already learned quite a bit about chord substitution in Chapter 3. Essentially, every example demonstrated some kind of chord substitution idea. Here, we'll get more in depth and clarify any questionable areas by learning *how* and *why* chords are extended and altered, as well as how a chord can be replaced by a better-sounding choice. Read and study this section often. Jazz masters know all of this information and have it at the tips of their fingers.

A Guide to Extension and Alteration

Triads and 7th chords become sonorous jazz harmonies through *extensions* (adding notes to a chord) and *alterations* (raising or lowering existing notes or extensions). The basic function of the chord does not change with these devices—every major chord is still a major chord whether it's C, C6 or Cmaj13♯11. A general rule is that any major chord-type can be used in place of another, as can any minor for minor, or dominant for dominant. That being said, here are some guidelines that reflect jazz common practice:

Chord Extensions

Chord extensions are generated from scales and modes. We know that the formula for a major triad is 1–3–5, so we take those corresponding notes from the major scale. To extend that chord, we simply add on more numbers (notes): 1–3–5–7 for a major 7th chord, 1–3–5–7–9 for a major 9th chord, etc. In this section, we'll apply these simple formulas for generating bigger chords from a multitude of scale and mode types. The idea is that each chord function implies a certain scale or mode. For example, in major keys:

I	Ionian (Major)
ii	Dorian
iii	Phrygian
IV	Lydian
V	Mixolydian
vi	Aeolian (Minor)
vii°	Locrian

Tonic Major (I)

The most common choices are from the harmonized major scale and almost always work.

6   6/9   maj7   maj9

Less common choices are from the harmonized Lydian mode (1–2–3–♯4–5–7), which gives us chords with a ♯11 (it's the same as ♯4). The Ionian ♭5 scale (1–2–3–4–♭5–6–7) and Lydian augmented scale (1–2–3–♯4–♯5–6–7) are other possibilities and generate chords with ♭5s, ♯5s, and ♯11ths. Even more dissonant possibilities include chords from the Lydian ♯2 scale (1–♯2–3–♯4–5–6–7), which gives us maj7♯9 chords. These harmonies might conflict with melodic lines, so be careful.

maj7♯11   maj7♯5   maj7♭5   maj7♯9

Subdominant (IV) or Other Major Chords

The most common choices are from the harmonized Lydian mode (the mode built on the 4th of the major scale) and almost always work.

6   6/9   maj7   maj9   maj7♯11

Less common choices are from the harmonized Lydian augmented scale (1–2–3–♯4–♯5–6–7), which generates chords with ♭5ths, ♯5ths, and ♯11ths. Even more dissonant possibilities include chords from the Lydian ♯2 scale (1–♯2–3–♯4–5–6–7), which gives us maj7♯9 chords. Again, these harmonies might conflict with melodic lines, so use your ears.

maj7♯5   maj7♭5   maj7♯9

Supertonic (ii) or Other Minor Chords

The most common choices for the ii chord (or minor chords other than iii and vi) are from the harmonized Dorian mode (1–2–♭3–4–5–6–♭7).

m6   m6/9   m7   m9

Submediant (iii) Minor Chords

The most common choices are from the harmonized Phrygian mode (1–♭2–♭3–4–5–♭6–♭7). Generally, diatonic 9th chords are not used, as most players don't care for the m7♭9 sound.

m6   m7   m7♭13

Mediant (vi) Minor Chords

The most common choices are from the harmonized Aeolian mode, the natural minor scale (1–2–♭3–4–5–♭6–♭7).

m7   m9   m7♭13

Tonic (i) Minor Chords

The most common choices are from the harmonic minor scale (1–2–♭3–4–5–♭6–7) and the melodic minor scale (1–2 ♭3–4–5–6–7). Some prefer the modal sound of the Dorian mode (1–2–♭3–4–5–6–♭7).

m   m6   m6/9   m(maj7)   m(maj9)   m7   m9

Dominant (V) Chords

The most common choices in major keys are from the Mixolydian mode (1–2–3–4–5–6–♭7).

$$7 \quad\quad 9 \quad\quad 11 \quad\quad 13 \quad\quad 7sus4 \quad\quad 9sus4$$

The most common choices in minor keys are from the altered dominant scale (1–♭2–♭3–♭4–♭5–♭6–♭7). These altered chords are also commonly used in major keys.

$$7♭5 \quad\quad 7♭9 \quad\quad 7♯9 \quad\quad 7♭13$$

Other common choices in major keys include the chords from the half/whole diminished scale (1–♭2–♭3–3–♯4–5–6–♭7).

$$7^{♯11}_{♭9} \quad\quad 13♭9 \quad\quad 13♯9$$

The Lydian ♭7 scale (1–2–3–♯4–5–6–♭7) is another possibility, especially for dominant-type chords that are *not* functioning as V chords.

$$7♯11 \quad\quad 9♯11 \quad\quad 13♯11$$

The Phrygian dominant scale (1–♭2–3–4–5–♭6–♭7) can create some modern-sounding dominant chords that work in major and minor keys.

$$11♭9 \quad\quad 7sus4♭9 \quad\quad 7sus4^{♭13}_{♭9}$$

The Purpose of Chord Substitution

The art of using substitute chords—essentially using one chord instead of another—is inexhaustible and something that the jazz masters have always been exploring. There are three main reasons most jazz players use substitutions.

1. To better harmonize a melody:
Much of the jazz repertoire is comprised of old pop songs and Broadway hits that were composed primarily between 1920 and 1960, songs that are typically called *standards*. Many standards have progressions that are quite good and only need slight changes to make them sound jazzier or more modern, but some need more drastic overhauls to be brought up to par. Some progressive jazz musicians want more modern sounds and will rework even strong progressions by applying contemporary harmonic logic. Listening to standards played by jazz masters and comparing and contrasting their changes to the original sheet music is the best way to study this approach.

2. To make a stronger solo section:
Some chord progressions work well with the composed melody, but might be too active (or not active enough) for effective solo sections. It is common to see sets of alternate changes for solos worked out by improvisers in today's jazz fake books. Listening to the melody harmonization played by jazz masters and comparing and contrasting their solo changes is the best way to study this approach.

3. To inspire soloists:
When comping for a soloist, it is your job to give him/her the best support possible. Frequently, this means that you will improvise chord substitutions based on what he/she is playing. You can either simplify, modify, or embellish the chord changes. Listening to how the jazz masters accompany a soloist on given recordings is the best way to study this approach.

That being said, we can distill much of what jazz musicians do to a handful of simple rules. The rules are only general guidelines—they reflect the approach jazz players might take in most situations. Whether or not these rules work depends mostly on the melodic structure of what's being played above the chords, be it a composed melody or an improvised solo. Use your ear and best musical judgment to determine if a rule works. Trial and error is the way to learn. After extensive experience applying the rules, you'll intuitively know what to do in any given musical situation.

The Ten Rules of Chord Substitution

Rule 1

Closely related chords (i.e., those that share common notes) can substitute for each other.
Example: A C triad can become an Em7 or Am7 chord.

Rule 2

A dominant-type chord can be preceded by its ii chord.
Example: G7 becomes Dm7–G7.

Rule 3

The iim7, iiim7, and vim7 chords can become dominant-type chords. This works especially well when the bass line is moving according to the circle of 5ths.
Example: Dm7 becomes D7.

Rule 4

Static harmonies can be embellished with diatonic harmonies. Sections of a harmonized scale moving in stepwise motion or some logical pattern often work well.
Example: Four bars of Cmaj7 become Cmaj7–Dm7–Em7–Dm7.

Rule 5

Short progressions can be used instead of simple harmony.
Example: C to G7 can become C—Am7—Dm7—G7.

Rule 6

Dominant-type chords can be replaced with the *tritone sub*. The most important notes of a dominant chord (the 3rd and ♭7) are also present in a dominant chord that's a tritone (three whole steps) away. The advantage is that the new chord has the sound of the ♭5th, ♭7th, ♭9th, plus the 3rd of the V chord.
Example: G7 (G–B–D–F) becomes D♭7 (D♭–F–A♭–C♭).

Rule 7

Dominant-type chords substitute for each other in minor 3rd relationships. A dominant chord built a minor 3rd higher contains the ♯9th, 5th, ♭7th, and ♭9th. A dominant chord built a minor 3rd lower contains the 13th, ♭9th, 3rd, and 5th.
Example: G7 (1–3–5–♭7) can become B♭7 (♯9–5–♭7–♭9), or E7 (13–♭9–3–5).

Rule 8

Leading tone diminished chords can be changed to altered dominant-type chords. A stronger root movement and more modern sound are created when the V7♭9 is used in place of vii°7. This works because of the common tones between the two chords.
Example: B°7 becomes G7♭9.

Rule 9

The iv6 is usually played as a iim7♭5 chord. Similarly, the IV6 is played as iim7. This works because of the common tones between the two chords.
Example: Fm6 becomes Dm7♭5.

Rule 10

A diminished chord (particularly with an added major 7th or 9th) built on the tonic note can be used to delay the resolution to the tonic.
Example: C°(maj7) can be used before Cmaj7.

Chapter 5: Full Progressions

This chapter explores the practical application of the previous materials to full-length progressions, including the blues form and jazz standards.

Blues

The 12-bar blues is the most common vehicle for jazz improvisation. The chart below shows the basic blues changes and some of the many possible substitutions that can be used. The changes are shown in the key of Bb, the most common key used by jazz players. The first row of changes is very close to the basic blues you might know from blues and rock styles, though it is actually similar to sets used by Thelonious Monk and Miles Davis. The second is a basic jazz blues—the real starting point. The third is a set of more advanced bebop changes used by Charlie Parker and others.

Bar 1			Bar 2			Bar 3		Bar 4
Bb9			Bb9 (or Eb9)			Bb9		Bb9
Bb9			Eb9			Bb9		Bb9
Bbmaj7	Am7b5	D7b9	Gm7			C9	Fm7	Bb9

Bar 5		Bar 6		Bar 7		Bar 8	
Eb9		Eb9		Bb9		Bb9	
Eb9		Eb9 (or Eb°7)		Bb9 (or Bb9/F)		Dm7	G7b9
Ebmaj7		Ebm7	Ab9	Dm7		Dbm7	G7b9

Bar 9		Bar 10		Bar 11		Bar 12	
F9		Eb9		Bb9		F9 (or Ab9)	
Cm7		F9		Bb9	G7b9	Cm7	F9
Cm7		F9		Dm7	Db9	Cm7	B9

B-flat Blues

Here is a set of voicings to use for a basic jazz blues in B♭. Notice how the ii–V progression figures prominently in the jazz version of the blues. Feel free to use a tritone sub in place of almost any dominant-type chord. These voicings are based on the top strings, leaving plenty of room for the bass player. The chord names in parenthesis above the frames show what a player *thinks* while creatively applying varied substitutions and extensions.

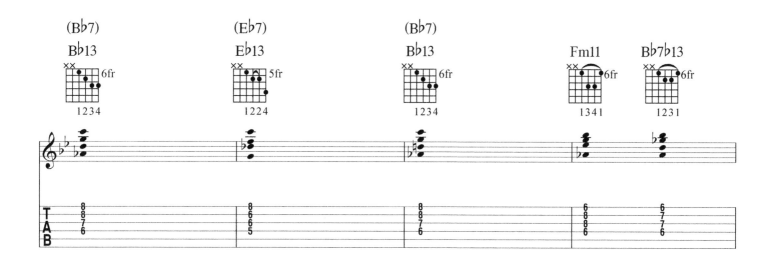

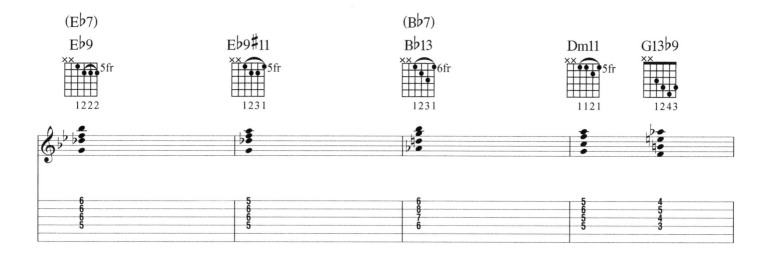

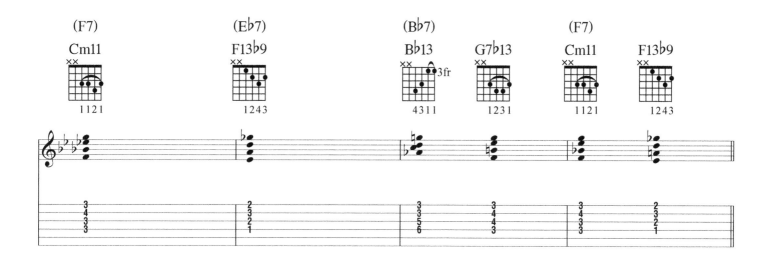

C minor Blues

The minor blues used in jazz usually stays fairly close to the following progression. It is common to turn the i chord into a dominant (V of iv) to emphasize the movement to the iv chord. The opening three bars illustrate a modern application of *Substitution Rule 4* from Chapter 4.

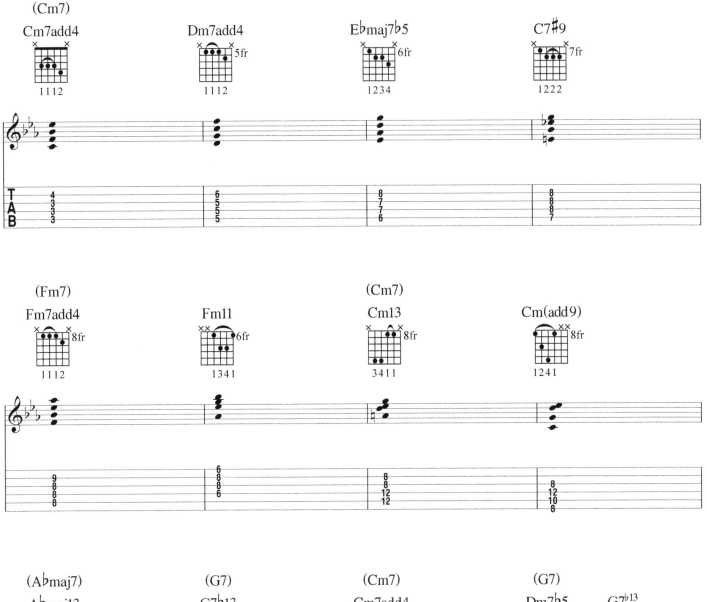

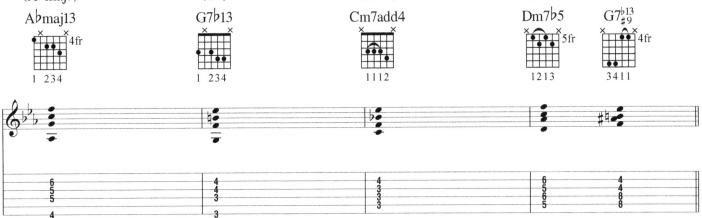

Autumn Left

These changes are quite simple, consisting primarily of ii–V–Is, in closely related major and minor key areas. With changes like these, it is easier for the player to focus on really making music, rather than navigating difficult progressions. The top row of chord symbols in parentheses represent what you might see in a fake book. The voicings demonstrate used demonstrate just a few of the dozens of possible approaches.

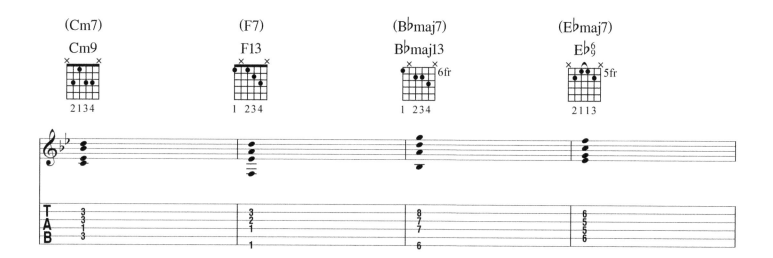

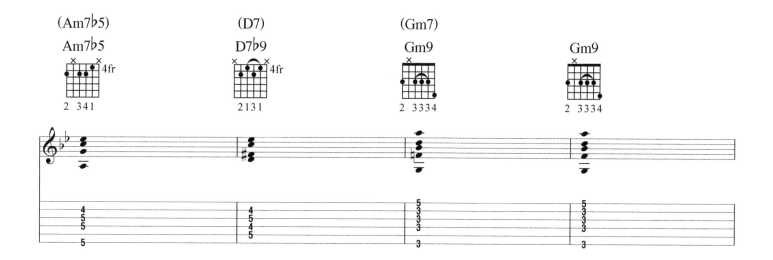

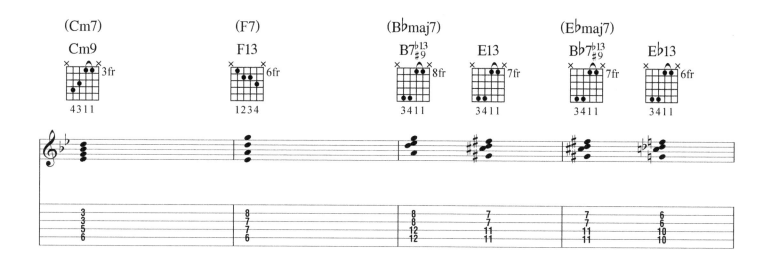

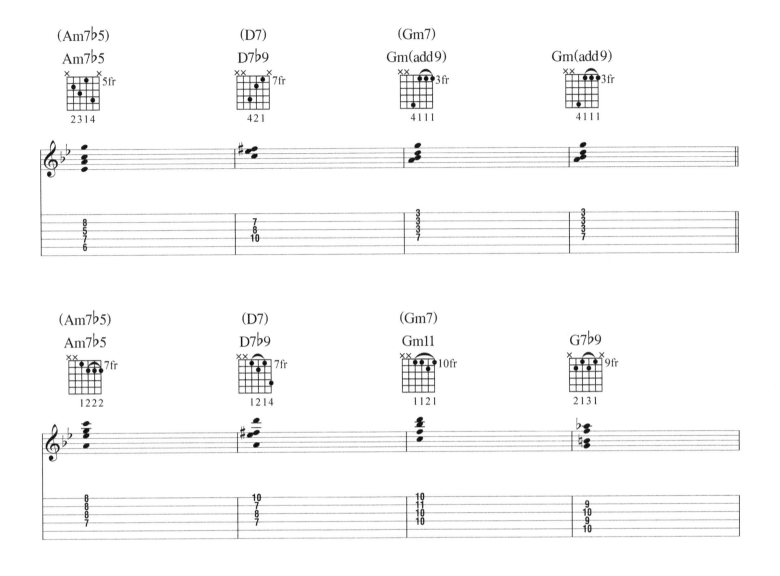

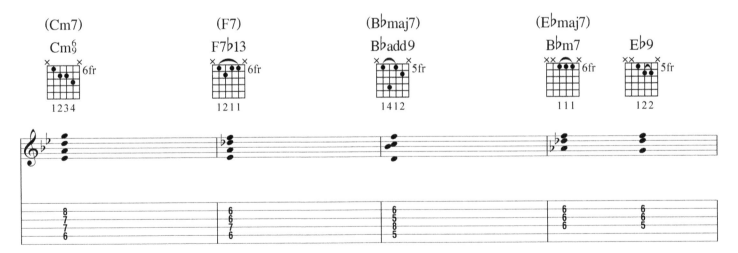

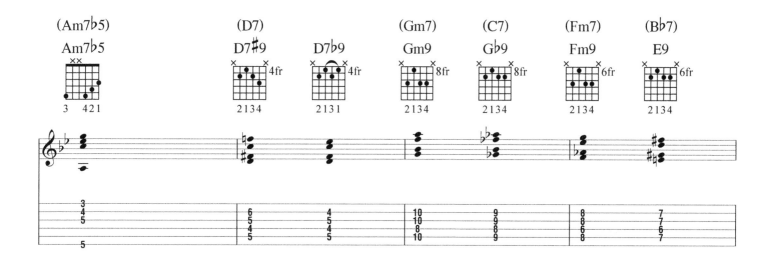

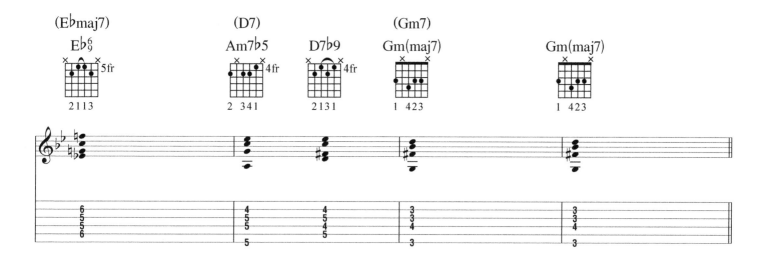

Bella by Barlight

This standard progression is a favorite among many jazz musicians for its variety of changes, particularly the different types of unresolved ii–Vs. The slow harmonic rhythm of the bridge—essentially two bars for each chord—makes for interesting chord substitution possibilities.

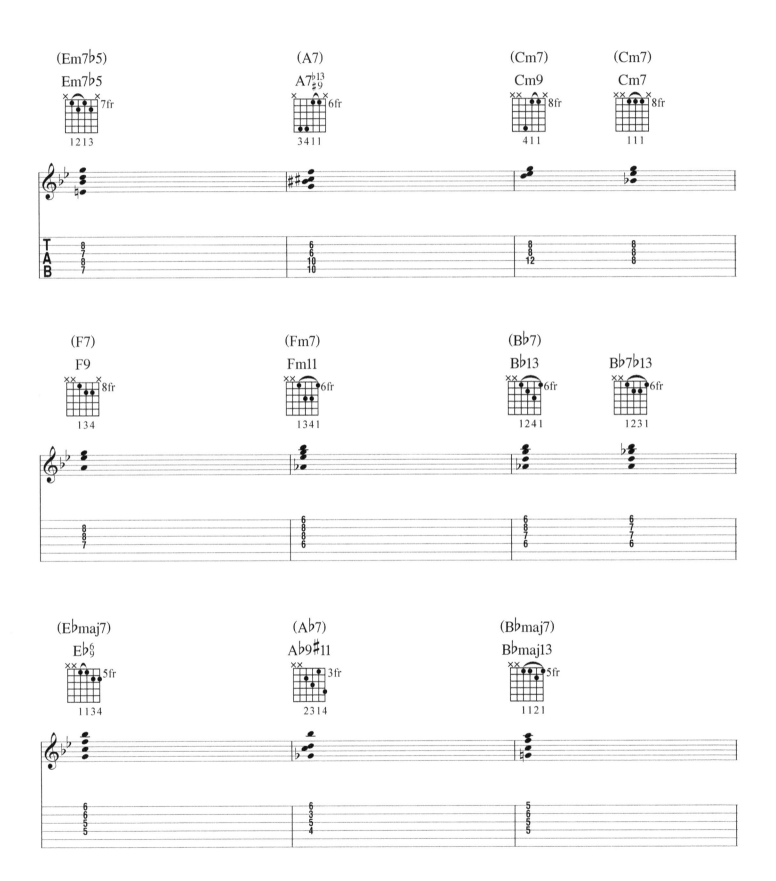

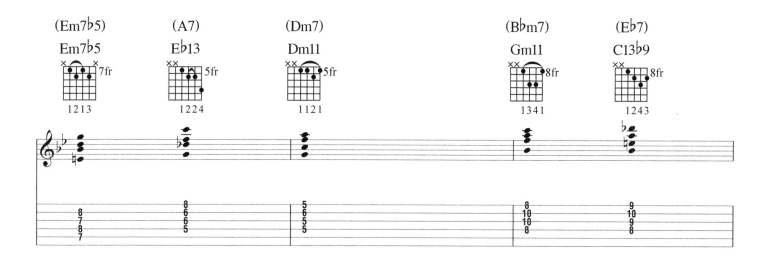

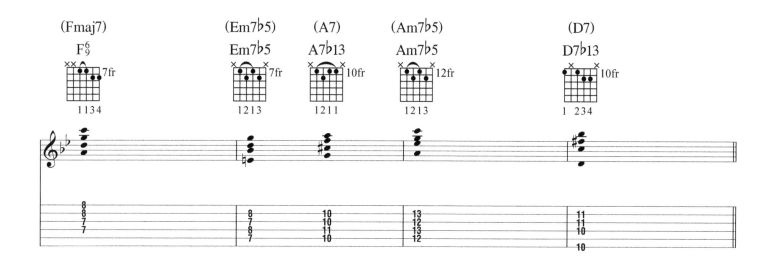

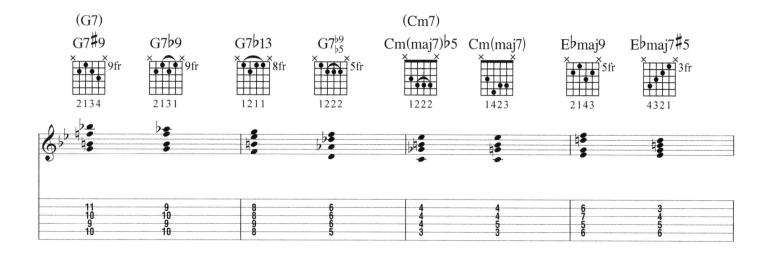

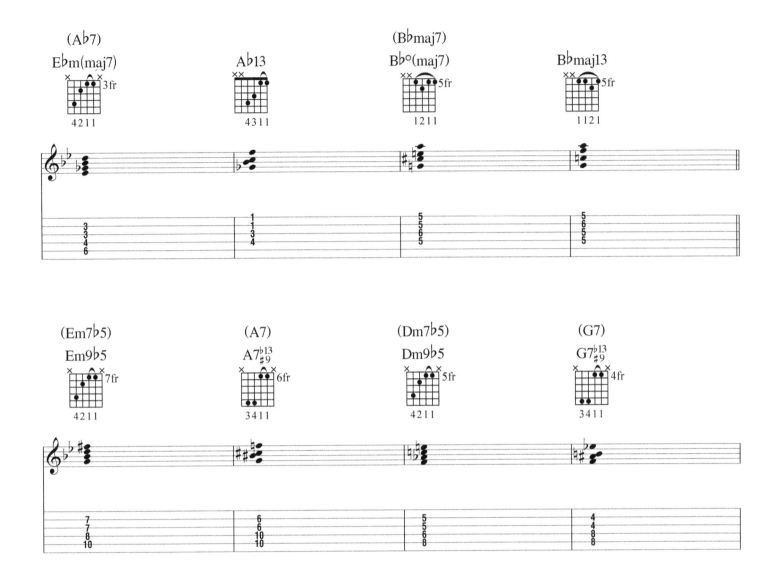

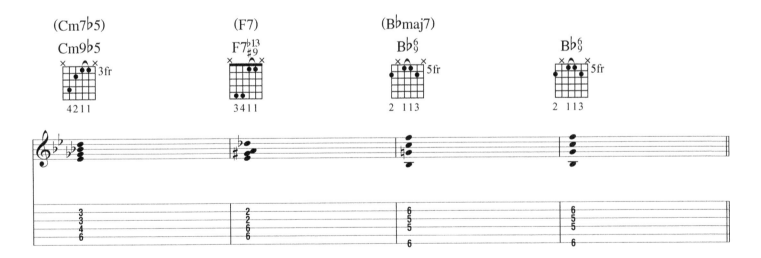

You Are All the Things

This is a common standard progression used throughout jazz history. Much of this progression's appeal is due to how the changes move through a number of distant key areas: Ab, C, Eb, G, and E. Again, the original changes are shown above in parentheses; play through them several times to get the basic sound in your head. The substitution and voicing approach is similar to that of guitarists Steve Khan and Mike Stern, originally based on the piano work of McCoy Tyner. The thinking behind this approach is to use quartal, or 4th-based voicings whenever possible, making sure the chords contain notes from (or extensions of) the underlying harmony, moving between chords in a melodic fashion. Pay particular attention to how a stack of perfect 4ths can imply a minor chord or major chord, depending on its context.

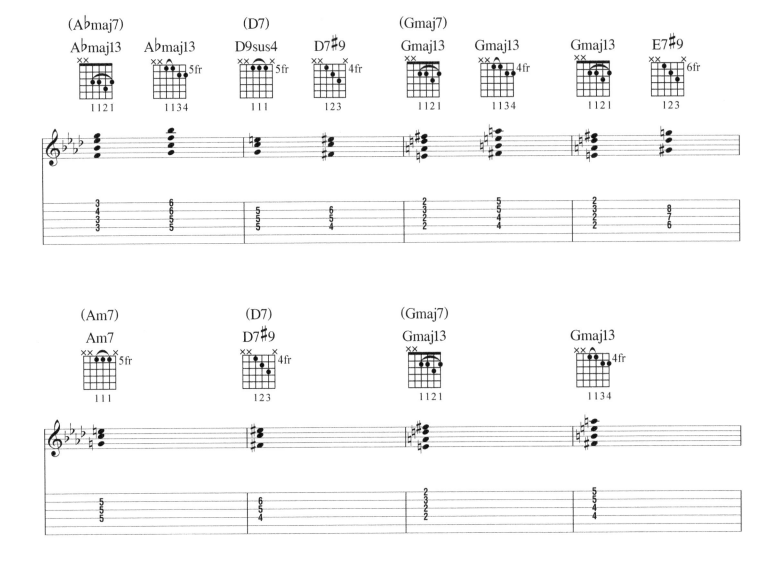

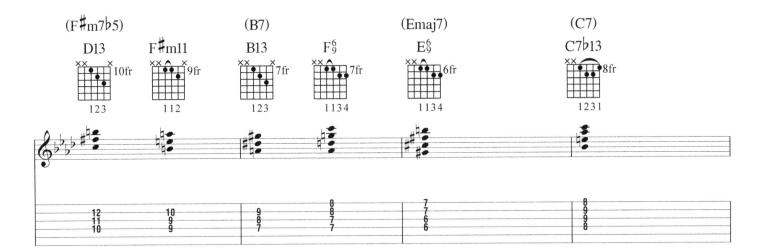

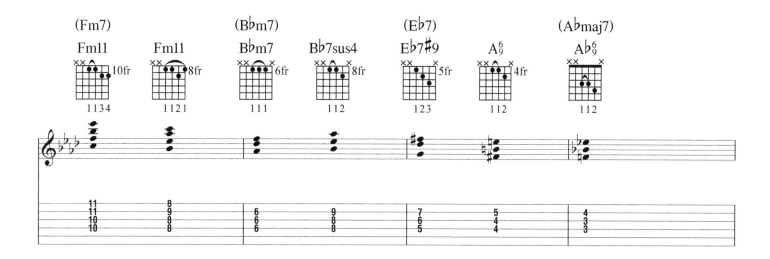

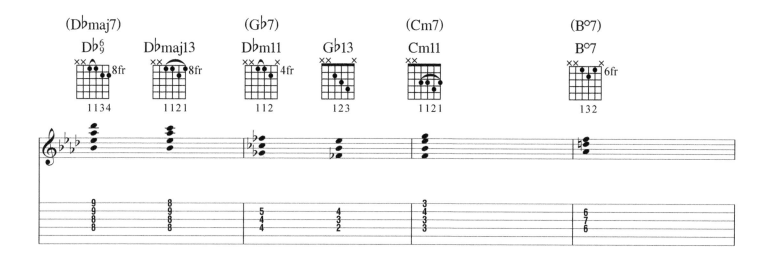

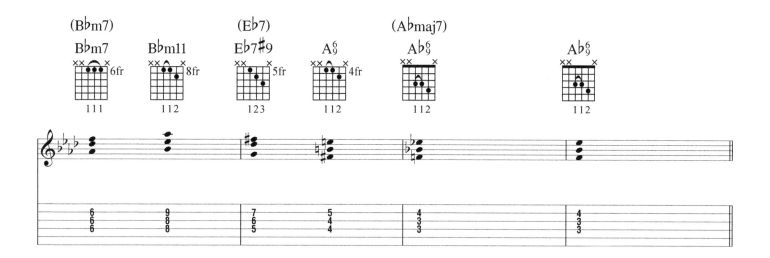

More Great Piano/Vocal Books

FROM CHERRY LANE

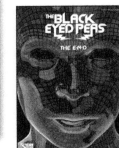

For a complete listing of Cherry Lane titles available,
including contents listings, please visit our web site at
www.cherrylane.com

See your local music dealer or contact:

Great DVD selections from CHERRY LANE

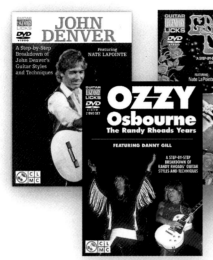

DVD

Steven Adler's Getting Started with Rock Drumming
taught by the Legendary Former Guns N' Roses Drummer!
02501387 DVD $19.99

Altered Tunings and Techniques for Modern Metal Guitar
taught by Rick Plunkett
02501457 DVD $16.99

Beginning Blues Guitar
RHYTHM AND SOLOS
taught by Al Ek
02501325 DVD $19.99

Black Label Society
featuring Danny Gill
Guitar Legendary Licks
02500983 2-DVD Set $19.99

Blues by the Bar
MORE AUTHENTIC LICKS BY THE BLUES MASTERS
taught by Danny Gill
02501477 DVD $16.99

Blues Masters by the Bar
taught by Dave Celentano
02501146 DVD $24.99

Children of Bodom
ALEXI LAIHO'S LEGENDARY LICKS
taught by Danny Gill
02501398 DVD $16.99

John Denver
featuring Nate LaPointe
Guitar Legendary Licks
02500917 DVD $16.99

Learn to Play the Songs of Bob Dylan
taught by Nate LaPointe
Guitar Legendary Licks
02500918 DVD $16.99

Funky Rhythm Guitar
taught by Buzz Feiten
02501393 DVD $24.99

Grateful Dead – Classic Songs
featuring Nate LaPointe
Guitar Legendary Licks
02500968 DVD $24.95

Grateful Dead
featuring Nate LaPointe
Guitar Legendary Licks
02500551 DVD $24.95

The Latin Funk Connection
02501417 DVD $16.99

Metallica – 1983-1988
featuring Doug Boduch
Bass Legendary Licks
02500481 DVD $16.99

Metallica – 1988-1997
featuring Doug Boduch
Bass Legendary Licks
02500484 DVD $16.99

Metallica – 1983-1988
featuring Nathan Kilen
Drum Legendary Licks
02500482 DVD $16.99

Metallica – 1988-1997
featuring Nathan Kilen
Drum Legendary Licks
02500485 DVD $16.99

Metallica – 1983-1988
featuring Doug Boduch
Guitar Legendary Licks
02500479 DVD $16.99

Metallica – 1988-1997
featuring Doug Boduch
Guitar Legendary Licks
02500480 DVD $24.99

Mastering the Modes for the Rock Guitarist
taught by Dave Celentano
02501449 DVD $19.99

Home Recording Magazine's 100 Recording Tips and Tricks
STRATEGIES AND SOLUTIONS FOR YOUR HOME STUDIO
02500509 DVD $16.99

Ozzy Osbourne – The Randy Rhoads Years
featuring Danny Gill
Guitar Legendary Licks
02501301 2-DVD Set $29.99

Pink Floyd – Learn the Songs from Dark Side of the Moon
by Nate LaPointe
Guitar Legendary Licks
02500919 DVD $16.99

Rock Harmonica
taught by Al Ek
02501475 DVD $16.99

Poncho Sanchez
featuring the Poncho Sanchez Latin Jazz Band
02500729 DVD $24.95

Joe Satriani
featuring Danny Gill
Guitar Legendary Licks Series
02500767 2-DVD Set $29.95

Joe Satriani – Classic Songs
featuring Danny Gill
Guitar Legendary Licks
02500913 2-DVD Set $29.95

Johnny Winter
taught by Al Ek
Guitar Legendary Licks
02501307 2-DVD Set 29.99

Johnny Winter
SLIDE GUITAR
featuring Johnny Winter with instruction by Al Ek
Guitar Legendary Licks
02501042 DVD $29.95

Wolfmother
featuring Danny Gill
02501062 DVD $16.99

See your local music retailer or contact

EXCLUSIVELY DISTRIBUTED BY

HAL•LEONARD® CORPORATION
7777 W. BLUEMOUND RD. P.O. BOX 13819 MILWAUKEE, WI 53213

Prices, contents, and availability subject to change without notice.

cherry lane
music company

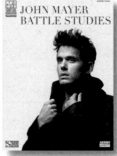